PAUL MERTON'S
HISTORY OF THE
TWENTIETH CENTURY

BⅫXTREE

*I dedicate this History of the 20th Century to my wife,
who's made me feel like I've lived through most of it.*

First published in Great Britain in 1993 by Boxtree Limted,
Broadwall House, 21 Broadwall, London SE1 9PL

All of the photographs used in this book were supplied by The Hulton Deutsch Collection Limited.

Paul Merton was photographed by Paul Forrester

Designed and reproduced by Blackjacks, London

Photo retouching by Rupert at Scanners, 081-579 3193

10 9 8 7 6 5 4 3 2 1

ISBN: 1 85283 570 2

A CIP catalogue entry for this book is available from the Britsh Library

Printed in Great Britain by Butler & Tanner Ltd, Frome and London

Introduction

The beginning of this sentence is now history. That's how history works. The moment you read the words "the moment", the moment has already gone. You may be familiar with the phrase, "History is written by the winning side"; well, this book is history for losers. This *History of the Twentieth Century* concentrates on the many untold stories of the past one hundred years.

Truth is a many-faceted concept and it has sometimes proved necessary to ignore so-called "facts" in order to delve deeper into the real stories behind well-known events. During the course of my extensive research I have been continually amazed by the number of momentous turning points throughout this century which have, until now, been completely ignored. Unfortunately, there has not been space in this book to include absolutely everything I've uncovered. I have, for example, skirted round the great brown suit scandal of the early '90s, although I do feel that people should be made aware of the phenomenon in order to stop the horror of brown suits ever happening again.

In writing this book I have used mainly English words and more often than not I have used them in a sensible consecutive order. This is also the way in which this book should be read – starting at the beginning and working through to the end. It is a continuous account and should be read as such. Various references in the 1950s, for example, will only make sense if you have first read the 1930s.

In choosing photographs I have generally used the side with the picture on it because this is usually more interesting than the other side which is blank. Any empty spaces you come across in this book, however, will undoubtedly be fascinating photographs that have been printed the wrong way round.

I do expect a certain amount of jealous criticism from professional historians who, I am sure, will describe my approach to writing this history as "making it up as you go along". I shall choose to ignore their petty quibbles.

And so, here, in consecutively written English words and outward facing photographs, is the true story of the 20th century. Happy reading.

PAUL MERTON

The 1900s: Recreation

The decade that was the 1900s was very much a transitional one. Some people were nervous about leaving the 19th century behind and argued that it had served them perfectly well for a hundred years and there was no pressing need for a change. Prophets of doom had predicted a time of disaster and certainly many prominent members of society were fearful of the future, none more so than Queen Victoria who had a life-altering experience in 1901. She died. She had reigned for 63 years and had won the nation's heart when her husband, Albert Memorial, passed on and left her a young widow. A young widow that she kept locked up in an airing cupboard. The passing of the old Queen seemed to mark the beginning of a new era. There were revolutionary changes in all aspects of society but perhaps the most surprising took place in the area of recreation. At the beginning of the 1900s people amused themselves in a whole variety of ways that now seem strange to our late twentieth century eyes. Nowadays

so much of our leisure time is taken up with television and assorted computer games, but in those far off golden days our ancestors found unlimited fun in ordinary simple objects. Like tables. As an example, just look at the two gentlemen in the picture **above.**

The eldest of the two seems relatively content to sit in a rather traditional pose and stare aimlessly into space. The younger gentleman, however, is far more energetic and is clearly having the time of his life by lying across the table in the most peculiar manner. This activity was known as "table sprawling" and was tremendously popular with the young men of the day, so much so that in 1904

A failed attempt to popularise chair leaning as an alternative to table sprawling.

In a moment of self doubt Queen Victoria attempts to strangle herself.

it was officially recognised as an Olympic status sport .

On the **right** we see the triumphant American team parading their winning table after their captain, George Disney, had successfully "sprawled" across it for more than thirty-eight minutes. It is regrettable that even in those days cheating was a major problem at the Olympic Games. The Spanish champion table sprawler, Julio Jaffa, was disqualified when it was discovered that he had achieved his record time of two hours and fourteen minutes mainly due to the fact that he was stone cold dead. He

was immediately banned for life. Although table sprawling was popular in its heyday, it could by no means be described as a sport of the people. Those who had tables were reluctant to spend all day sprawling across them, while the poorer elements of society had no tables at all. It was common practice in those days for the lower classes to nail their food to the wall. A familiar sound in the

A potentially lethal weapon is abandoned during the Boer War when dozens of trained soldiers completely fail to understand how to use it.

Winston Churchill and the Kaiser meet on a blind date when test trials carried out by the world's first dating agency go disastrously wrong. They reportedly spent a rather awkward evening at the cinema.

East End of London was that of a six inch nail being driven into a jacket potato. The noted sociologist Dr Alan Pub spent some time in the Whitechapel area studying this phenomenon and later wrote about it in his acclaimed book *I've Seen People Nail Their Dinner To The Wall*. The following is an extract . . .

"The Cockney takes a great deal of pride in his ability to affix a family meal to solid brickwork. It seems a perfectly sensible idea and it certainly keeps their food off the floor. Even during this difficult time the Cockney's spirit is alive and well."

The difficult time to which Pub refers is the famous wood drought of 1905. It seems inconceivable to us now, but there was a severe shortage of wood in the early years of this century. Recent research indicates that this was entirely due to

Early Developments – The Motor Car

(left)
Taxi-drivers road test the latest model. The design is later scrapped after drivers complain that it's "Ruddy stupid".

(below)
Mrs Elizabeth Coppell, the inventor of the beaded car seat cover, hard at work in her luxurious factory.

the then prevalent fashion for titled gentlemen to wear wooden wigs. A tremendous scandal was narrowly avoided when the Duke of Devonshire ordered thirty acres of forest to be cut down in order to supply him with a giant quiff for the Lord Mayor's banquet. The government of the day declared a state of emergency and banned all wood fires as well as savagely cutting the average contents of a box of matches. People were urged to avoid using wood products wherever possible and Edward VII showed a fine example by making a fence out of pheasants (**right**).

Once the lower classes realised that the reason they couldn't have proper fires was because the toffs loved wearing wooden wigs there were full-scale riots. The police had tremendous difficulty in dealing with the hostile crowds because they had run out of wooden batons and had to resort to flicking wet towels across the back of the demonstrators' legs. The wood drought lasted for three years and eventually killed off table sprawling as a competitive sport.

The 1908 Olympics saw the emergence of an entirely new sporting discipline that had the advantage of needing no specialised equipment. The sport was called pointing.

In the picture **below** we see the British Ladies Synchronised Pointing squad exercising the exceedingly difficult backwards double point manoeuvre.

Incidentally, the ladies holding the outstretched feet are purely a safety measure in case any of the competitors topple backwards through over-enthusiastic pointing. The woman in the hat is a groupie. During these Olympic games Britain enjoyed a certain advantage. Many other countries refused to enter because they considered it mad to point. The Canadians however brushed aside all considerations of genteel etiquette and were desperately unlucky not to win more than a handful of bronze medals. The picture **below** is a rare study of the Canadian

Fran Potterton demonstrating her highly individual Potterton Point. This photograph may not be of the highest quality, but in many ways we are lucky to see it at all. It was long thought lost and only re-appeared in 1985 when it was found in the belly of a shark caught off the coast of Brazil. The 1908 games were a

personal triumph for Fran and she was a tragic loss to the sport when she was killed while attempting to point against doctors orders. These Olympics quickly established pointing as the national pastime. Unlike table sprawling everybody had the ability to point and the newly-emerged British film industry was quick to jump on the bandwagon. **Below** is a still from the now forgotten film, *I'm Off*, which was made in 1909. In the depicted scene our hero is attempting to comfort his loved one before he leaves for battle. She is distraught for two reasons. Firstly, she knows that her man is off to war, and secondly, she has just learned that the beautiful countryside outside her front door is, in fact, painted onto cloth. The original caption to this picture reads *"I'll have one more point before I go."* The music hall entertainer Gus Sweeney became enormously popular during these years with a highly original stage act that consisted of him suddenly pointing at totally unexpected angles.

Is this a genuine photograph of a spirit from beyond the grave or three nutters with access to a camera?

During a lull in the 1908 Olympics Mr Christian De Witt amuses the crowd by reading extracts from the collected works of Lord Byron through an inaudible megaphone.

In a newspaper interview published in the now defunct *Daily Rubbish*, George attempted to explain the appeal of his unusual act.

"I am constantly amazed by the extraordinary reaction that my performances engender in the British public. On a good night the audience will bellow out requests for their favourite angles. During one particular show at the Hackney Empire a rather well-to-do young lady suddenly surprised her chaperone with a passionate plea for a point that was thirty-three degrees off the perpendicular. Naturally, I complied and judging by her enthusiastic applause my simple efforts were well appreciated. She was later escorted to my dressing room where she thanked me profusely for acceding to her request. With tear-filled eyes she explained that thirty-three degrees had a special place in her affections because it was the exact angle that

The Olympics committee, who were not impressed by Mr De Witt's efforts, replace him with a gramophone that successfully plays a selection of mood music through an inaudible loudspeaker.

her poor papa had been buried at. I am not a man who feels at ease with public displays of emotion so I asked the stage doorman to throw her out."

Such was the enormous popularity of the new sport that religious groups called for its banning on the grounds that people were clearly enjoying themselves. Its most outspoken critic was Mrs Elizabeth Munroe, who argued that the human arm was not designed to be held aloft for excessively long periods. Furthermore, she believed that the practice would lead to blood draining into

The very first documented acid house rave.

An obsessive pointer gets up deliberately at 3.30 in the morning to indulge in a solitary point.

people's heads until they were three times their normal size. The picture **above** is a clear illustration of her deeply held fears. Mrs Munroe claimed that people with inflated heads would be more likely to pull grotesque faces in the street. *"It's an ideal opportunity for professional face pullers to enhance their already hideous practises,"* she wrote in a letter to *The Times*. However, Mrs Munroe's self-appointed position as the nation's moral guardian was severely undermined when it was later revealed that she had secretly married a turnip. Although her more hysterical arguments could be easily dismissed as the ravings of a mad woman, it's clear in retrospect that pointing also had a far more sinister aspect than anyone in the 1900s would ever have dreamed of. This subject will be further discussed in due course. As a final footnote it cannot be considered entirely coincidental that the world's first under-arm deodorant was developed in 1910.

The 1910s: Oh Really

The 1910s were very much a decade of transition. Those people who had originally been so nervous about entering the 20th century now argued that, although the 1900s had been fine, there was little point in the world pushing its luck any further. A campaign was mounted by the "Bring Back The 19th Century Society" who eventually found an M.P. willing to argue their case in the House of Commons. The M.P., Sir Gregory Balloon, was later completely discredited when it was revealed that he had secretly bought a job lot of 1810 calendars and that he stood to make a personal fortune should the year ever come round again. As a personal tribute to his mother, Queen Victoria, who died at the beginning of the 1900s,

The Russian Royal Family enjoying a quiet weekend. It was this type of behaviour that led inevitably to a bloody revolution.

Edward VII decided to die at the beginning of the 1910s. The Prime Minister, Mr Asquith, spoke for the nation when he described King Edward as "not only a great monarch but also a tremendous potato." When George V was crowned

In a last ditch effort to stave off defeat at the hands of the Bolsheviks, Rasputin attempts to curry favour with the Moscow branch of the Women's Institute.

the following year he made a solemn promise to do his best to die in the early 1920s. Compared to the devil-may-care spirit of the previous decade the 1910s were terrifically gloomy. When the Titanic made its maiden voyage in 1912 none of the passengers on board realised their stupidity in buying return tickets. Although the ship will always be remembered for its dramatic sinking we should also take note of its extraordinary design. At the time it was the longest ship ever built. The chief designer, Pat Nuisance, explained the thinking behind the unusual length in a candid interview with *Iceberg Weekly* in 1938. "Initially I designed the Titanic to be more than 650 miles long. I thought it might appeal to people to travel on a ship that was already half-way to New York before it set sail." Later in the same interview Mr Nuisance revealed a rather callous attitude towards the safety of the passengers. "People criticised me for not providing enough lifeboats in the original design. But there was nothing to stop passengers bringing their own lifeboats with them. In my experience people display a rather greedy side to their character once they're on board ship. They make constant demands. 'Where's my dinner?' 'Where's my tea?' 'Where's my lifeboat?' Honestly, some people expect everything to be provided for them. At the official inquiry I was heavily criticised for leaping into the first available lifeboat. Well, I'm a very superstitious man. I thought if I stayed on board it might bring me bad luck."

The Suffragette movement grew ever stronger in the 1910s as women became increasingly more radical in their pursuit of the right to

Horatio Beadle tests the world's first camcorder in 1913. Mr Beadle was convinced that people would want to view their own recordings on their television sets and was bitterly disappointed to discover that television sets had not yet been invented.

George Dull, the notorious man of a thousand faces, makes an early appearance as "bearded man with cap." We shall hear more of him later.

vote. The Sarcasm Campaign of 1914 certainly touched a raw nerve within the corridors of power. The idea behind the campaign was a simple one. Whenever the Prime Minister addressed the House of Commons groups of women packed into the public gallery would greet his every utterance with the words, *"Oh really."* This behaviour so outraged M.P.s they passed an emergency law banning the use of the phrase in public places. The Suffragettes neatly side-stepped this ridiculous ruling by changing the pronunciation to *"Oh weally."* A further law was

Above: *The Royal Navy's dreadnought, HMS Enormous, pulls alongside the extremely long and extremely doomed Titanic.*

Von Hindenburg, a high ranking German officer, considerately points out the edge of the map to Kaiser Wilhelm

introduced making it illegal to utter any words that in any way sounded like "Oh really." This move totally backfired when an Irish lawyer called O'Reilly successfully sued the government for making it illegal for him to pronounce his own name in public. One of the most fervent opponents of the Suffragettes was the newspaper publisher Henry Lido. He refused to acknowledge the existence of women at all and claimed that they were really men who simply dressed up in funny clothes for a lark. In one particularly passionate editorial he declared, *"that it would be as ridiculous to grant votes to these*

The German army's efforts to camouflage themselves as tree bark were never entirely successful.

so-called women as it would be to stop five year old boys working down the mines or to believe that one day music could be reproduced in a digital form with laser optics reading encoded information on small silver discs." The Suffragette movement received a tremendous boost in 1916 when Mrs Melissa Etheridge successfully chained herself to George V.

The German Army's ingenious trench cutter shortly before it went berserk and dug a trench 840 miles long across mainland Europe. The French later used the trench to form part of their underground railway system.

The 1910s were, of course, dominated by the Great War which was to prove a human tragedy on a massive scale. At the outbreak of hostilities in 1914 Field Marshal Sir John French confidently declared that the fighting would be over by Christmas. Unfortunately, he didn't specify which Christmas. At the beginning of the war a great deal of naivety was displayed by both sides When the Belgian Government issued bicycles to its Army (**below**) it honestly believed that it had

discovered a wonderful new military tactic. "A bicycle is not a horse," reasoned the Belgian Prime Minister, Mr Toms. For some odd reason this rather obvious remark was greeted by the Belgian people as a wonderfully insightful observation. It was frequently heard at the more fashionable dinner parties and soon the Prime Minister was urged to come up with more of the same. "A hat is not a tree" was greeted with wild enthusiasm but many observers felt that his master-piece was the rather curious phrase, "Tulips don't eat meat." Long after the war was over Mr Toms enjoyed a lucrative career writing those strange slogans often found in Christmas crackers. However, we mustn't lose sight of the fact that the Belgian Cycle Army was severely routed in its first military engagement when it was ambushed by the German Cycle Army (**right**) hiding in some nearby woods. It must be said that the British were so supremely con-fident of victory that many generals wondered if there was any need to

actually turn up for the fighting. The arrogance of such regiments as the King's Own Toffs is clearly shown in the photographic study **above**. The Toffs believed that fighting during the day was all very well as long as it didn't interfere with their own private dinner arrangements. The Germans on the other hand

took the war far more seriously and right from the beginning were constantly experimenting with new technology. Unfortunately for them, their ideas committee consisted entirely of habitual drug users (**right**) who were forever inventing things that seemed to have no practical purpose. The German high command were astonished when the extraordinary contraption shown **opposite** was presented to them in 1916. And they were none too pleased when the ideas committee collapsed into hysterical laughter whenever they tried to explain its function. Their anger was

nothing compared to the rage that gripped the German Flying Ace, Baron Von Morrison, when he was presented with the committee's revolutionary new aero-plane design (**below**). From secret papers only recently discovered it's clear that the Baron had very little time for the ideas committee who he described

During the heat of battle, cocktail shakers are delivered to high ranking officers.

as "a bunch of cannabis smoking wretches who spend all day dressed up like Arabs." When the newspaper baron Henry Lido saw the photograph he claimed that it was simply a bunch of women with facial hair problems. As strange as it may seem, some elements within the British Government were actually highly impressed with the committee's ideas and attempted to emulate the Germans by holding top secret "Come as a Nutcase" evenings (a particularly lively example is shown **below**). Various schemes were generated by these bizarre gatherings. All of which proved to be entirely useless. Among the more ludicrous suggestions was the idea that everybody in Britain should be dipped in special invisible paint so if the Germans did invade they wouldn't be able to find anybody. Actual plans were drawn up and

ready to be put into operation until one bright spark at the War Office queried the existence of this special invisible paint. He refused to be fobbed off with the argument that as the paint was invisible it was notoriously hard to find but there was certainly some around somewhere. Perhaps the greatest error was to employ the notorious eccentric Mavis Doolally as a secret agent. She was particularly unsuitable for the job because she was already world famous for competing at Wimbledon with a stringless racket (**right**). She was eventually arrested in 1917 while trying to persuade the Kaiser to sign a piece of paper with the words "I surrender" written on it. Perhaps one of the very few positive aspects of a war that killed ten million people was that finally in 1918 women were allowed to vote for the first time in a British General Election. Their valuable war work in factories and other important areas of production meant that the Government could no longer delay the inevitable. Votes for women became a reality. Henry Lido committed suicide. His wife, upon being told the news, reacted with the two simple words, *"Oh really."*

Here we see plucky British girls hard at work making a communal hat modelled on their own distinctive gear.

The 1920s:
The Modern Age

As a decade the 1920s certainly had some transition but perhaps not as much as the 1910s. The "Bring Back The 19th Century Society" was officially disbanded in 1922 when it became clear to even their most die-hard supporters that they were on a losing streak. Perhaps the Society's Chairman, Hubert Tube, said it best when he told a packed press conference, "We are on a losing streak."

At the beginning of the 1920's the British public instinctively gathered outside the gates of Buckingham Palace to await the inevitable news of the death of the King. The profits of the black armband manufacturers trebled as people prepared themselves for the worst. Grown men were seen to be embracing in the street, too emotional to speak. However, it soon became clear that everything was not right with the Monarch.

Adapting to modern times, Chief Crazy-Horse changes his name to Chief One-Careful-Owner.

A scandal quickly erupted when George V actually refused to die at the beginning of the new decade as he had earlier promised. He acknowledged that he was breaking with Royal tradition but argued that he only did so on the grounds that he couldn't help it. He also claimed that he had a duty to continue living because he was still chained to Mrs Melissa Etheridge (**above**) and he would not wish to inconvenience her any more than was strictly necessary. The public was distraught.

The King's continued good health upset a great many people who felt that the start of a new decade wouldn't be the same without a bumper Royal funeral. The newspapers of the day carried regular bulletins that were avidly read by the public eager for the latest news. *The Daily Sketch* sold out within hours when its front page carried the headline "WORST FEARS CONFIRMED – KING GOES WATER SKIING." Such was the intensity of

Women everywhere were fascinated by the contents of Rudolph Valentino's nostrils.

criticism that the King felt obliged to put across his side of the story. He was clearly unrepentant when he told a packed press conference, "We are entering an exciting modern age and so, consequently, I do not intend to die until 1936, at the earliest. And, even then, I might go on a bit longer!"

Unfortunately, due to an administrative error, the King's press conference was held in the same room, at the same time, as the "Bring Back The 19th Century Society's" press conference. Sub-sequently, the next day's newspapers carried a rather garbled version of the day's events. Until now it has been believed that in answer to the question, "Do you accept that your continued existence is severely undermining the

Leonard Beale, the world's biggest man, demonstrates his difficulty in using public transport.

Winston Churchill entertaining his hunting friends with a quick tune on the harmonica. Unbeknown to them, it was a specially hollowed-out harmonica filled with gin. Consequently, he spent more time swallowing than blowing.

status of the Monarchy?", the King replied, "Look, if you're taking the piss I'm going home." However, after close inspection of the original transcript, it can now be confirmed that these words should have been properly attributed to Mr Tube.

On April 9th, 1923, Katy Emily Jones was born. I record this fact not because she plays a pivotal role in the history of the 20th Century but because she is my mother-in-law and I want to keep in with the family.

His Majesty was quite correct, of course, when he predicted the arrival of an exciting modern age. Perhaps taking their lead from the German Ideas Committee in the Great War, the inventors of the world worked non-stop on a

A group of casual ramblers indulging in the joy of pointing.

Harry Houdini, the famous escapologist and contortionist, demonstrating the notoriously difficult "out of focus" point.

A Personal Guide to Pointing

Pointing as a pleasurable pastime has lost none of its attraction over the years. Anyone can point. It's not at all odd. Apart from the more advanced techniques, pointing requires no complicated safety equipment and it's not weird. No one would think it strange if you were discreetly to practise the manoeuvres illustrated below in front of the mirror in the privacy of your own bathroom. Just don't forget to lock the door.

The Lord Kitchener "Your Country Needs You" All Purpose Point. *Ideal for beginners. Notice how my finger seems to follow you around the room.*

The Standard "Gun Dog" Point. *Particularly useful for pointing over long distances.*

The "Lunar Urchin" Point. *Used mainly for pointing out the moon to small children and pointing out small children to the moon.*

The Cranium Point. *Potentially dangerous and not to be attempted by novices or those of a nervous disposition. One small slip and you can have your eye out.*

The "Nasty Niff" Point. *An essential point for identifying the source of offensive odours. Also comes in handy underwater.*

The Pocket Point. *Readers should note that this point still constitutes an offense in Scotland.*

The "Addicts" Point. *Despite heavy medication the addict will persist in trying "just a small one" in the mistaken belief that he can handle it. This practise is strongly discouraged by Pointers Anonymous.*

The Double Digit Point. *A rather esoteric manoeuvre which serves no useful purpose whatsoever.*

The Ultimate Triple Point. *It is impossible to point more than this with all your clothes on.*

variety of new ideas. It is surprising to realise just how many modern day contraptions were originally developed in the 1920s. As an example, the very first mobile phone was invented by Mrs Felicity Solicitor in 1922 (an early publicity shot is shown **right**) From our perspective it perhaps looks rather cumbersome. The motor bike is an essential part of the design because the huge battery necessary to power the phone is cleverly disguised as the side car. This inherent design fault made it very difficult to use the phone in the back of a taxi. After an exhaustive trial period, many other drawbacks were highlighted. The receiver was extremely heavy and so, whenever it was

picked up, it would unbalance the motor cyclist to such an extent that he would immediately fall off. Every time Mrs Solicitor was phoned the caller would hear her say "Hello," immediately followed by the sound of crashing metal and moaning. As soon as the word got round, Mrs Solicitor, who had a great many enemies, was telephoned fifteen to twenty times a day. She stubbornly refused to acknowledge this basic fault and insisted that she enjoyed crashing because it was, "a marvellous way of meeting new people."

Undoubtedly, the most prolific inventor of the 1920's was the extraordinary Victor Speed-Boat. Not only was he blessed with boundless energy, but he also had a unique vision that continually led him into uncharted areas of innovation. Unfortunately, the main reason why these areas were uncharted was because nobody else particularly wanted to go there. It was Speed-Boat's curse that every single one of his inventions was considered completely useless. One of his earliest ideas was the 'Speed-Boat All-Electrical Washing Machine' (**right**). His high hopes for the marketing of this new product were severely dashed when the Royal Society of Inventors described it as, "a simple bucket with a useless chunk of metal stuck on the top." Undeterred, Victor threw himself back into his work and soon developed the 'Speed-Boat All-Electric Potato Peeler' (**opposite, top right**). This idea never got off the ground due to the chronic shortage of all-electric potatoes. Still defiantly undeterred, he retaliated with what I believe was his finest invention. Although

the vacuum-cleaner had already been developed elsewhere, it was Victor who devised the astonishing 'Speed-Boat All-Purpose Pet Propeller' (**below**). Here we see it in operation. The idea was a simple one. The following is a quote from the original patent, *"'The Speed-Boat All-Purpose Pet Propeller' is solely designed to keep the family pet amused while Mother cleans the carpet. A powerful jet of warm*

air maintains the pet at an average height of three feet, thus ensuring that no animal will ever again feel ignored during the completion of necessary house work."

Initially, the idea was greeted with some enthusiasm. It was Speed-Boat's sheer bad luck, however, that his 'All-Purpose Pet Propeller' was never taken up by a manufacturer. Extensive trials were carried out and for a while the device seemed to live up to its expectations. Disaster struck however, when a French Poodle was mistakenly placed in an air stream

previously set for an Irish Wolf Hound. The resulting blast sent the startled animal crashing through the ceiling. Although the dog was unharmed the man in the upstairs flat suffered a minor heart attack when the French Poodle hurtled

Lenin tells the assembled crowd that all Russians should work together for the glory of the revolution – and can they make a start by pumping his back tyre up?

An early meeting of the Tory Party's 1922 Committee is dispersed by Lloyd George in drag.

through his floorboards at eighty-five miles an hour. After this unfortunate incident the 'Speed-Boat All-Purpose Pet Propeller' was officially declared a hazard to dogs, ceilings and men upstairs. Such a turn of events might have persuaded a lesser man to concentrate on more obviously practical ideas. Not Victor Speed-Boat. He committed suicide. Ironically, his grandson, Lewis Speed-Boat, also an inventor, later achieved the distinction of inventing a machine that carried his own name and is still in popular use today. It is, of course, the Lewis Trumpet used in Symphony Orchestras around the world.

The 1920s were confirmed as the age of discovery as early as 1922, when Tutankhamun's Tomb was unearthed (the actual opening of the tomb is shown **right**). Despite warnings of an ancient curse, archaeologists were tremendously excited by the find. The leader of the expedition, Howard Carter, was typically blasé about the supposed evil consequences that would beset anyone daring to enter the tomb. He told the world's journalists at a packed press conference that, "the hieroglyphics referring to this curse are so ridiculously fanciful that no serious minded investigator would allow himself to be troubled by it for a single moment. For example, as leader of this expedition, I will apparently soon be transformed into a bizarre half-man, half-horse creature. I do not intend to take this threat seriously." Unfortunately, due to an administrative error, Mr Carter's

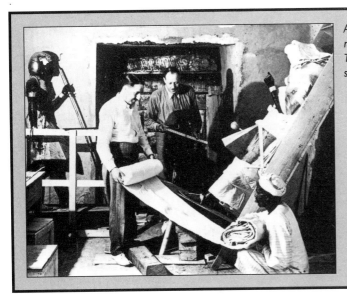

Archeologists rolling up Tutankhamun's sleeping bag.

press conference was held in the same room at the same time as the King's press conference, and the "Bring Back The 19th Century Society's" press conference. Contrary to contemporary reports, it is now clear that Mr Carter did not respond to the question, "Just how important is this find?" with the words, "Look, if you're taking the piss I'm going home." It seems that Hubert Tube spent the entire conference endlessly repeating this phrase. So far, investigations have failed to determine the exact time that Mr Tube did eventually go home. If Howard Carter's words had received wide-spread publicity there would not have been such universal astonishment in 1929 when he was regularly seen galloping home through the park politely wiping up the unsightly and maloderous mess he tended to deposit on the footpaths (**above**).

Despite tragedies such as these, by the end of the '20s, nobody was in any doubt that the Modern Age had well and truly arrived.

Walt Disney creates a new character called Mickey Mouse. Despite thousands of letters begging him to stop, Disney perseveres with a tiresome series of films starring the screeching, cretinous little rodent.

The 1930s: Baldwin's Shadow

The 1930s were a period of transition only in the sense that without them there would have been a very awkward gap between the 20s and the 40s.

By the beginning of the decade the British public were so heartily sick of George V that continuing news of his good health was greeted with a rather resigned shrug of the shoulders. The King, however, redeemed himself in the eyes of many people when he eventually decided to die, as he had earlier predicted, in 1936. This placed Mrs Melissa Etheridge in a rather delicate position.

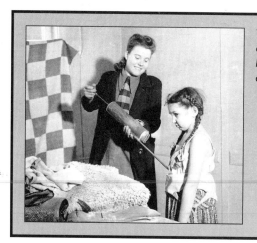

The world's first experiments in liposuction are carried out.

New tunnels built for London transport's Piccadilly Line are rejected when it is realised that they're too small and not underground.

Top secret tests are carried out to discover if it's possible to see through wood.

Still chained to the King, she was reluctant to relinquish what for her had become a rather privileged position. As she told the *Daily Nonsense* in an exclusive interview immediately after the King's demise, *"I have enjoyed meeting exciting people from all walks of life. At first it was difficult to tell if His Majesty was hostile towards me because whenever I attempted to strike up a conversation he set the dogs onto me. I believe, however, that over the years he gradually began to tolerate my presence and I don't believe I'm being too fanciful when I say that towards the end he came to look upon me as a woman who was permanently chained to his upper body."* The government of the day solved the rather difficult problem of what to do with Mrs Etheridge by promising her that she could chain herself to the Duke of Devonshire if she allowed herself to be unchained from the King. This she agreed to do. She was absolutely furious when she discovered that the Duke of Devonshire was a pub in the Old Kent Road but she nevertheless chained herself to it anyway. Her last years were spent attempting to tell hardened drinkers all about the time George V burped during a Royal Command Performance and tried to blame it on her. "Al Jolson knew it wasn't me," she would tell the assembled boozers, "but he was too much of a gentleman to say so." In his autobiography *A Tin Of Boot Polish and a Loud Voice Got Me Where I Am Today*, Jolson refutes this version of events. *"I once performed at the London Palladium, yes sir, by command of George V. What a guy. He had*

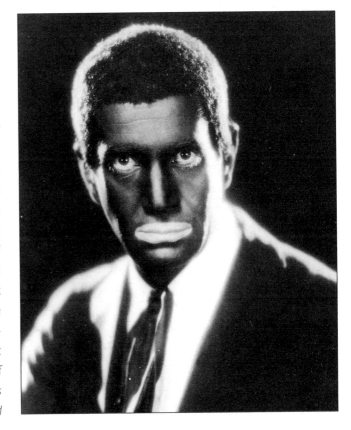

some crazy dame with him who nearly ruined the show by burping throughout my performance. She tried to blame him with some cock-eyed story about His Majesty working in a new ventriloquist act. I wasn't fooled, no sir." Why exactly Mr Jolson chose to write his autobiography in this rather third-rate parody of American speech patterns remains a mystery. When Mrs Etheridge heard that Jolson had denied her story she attempted to sell her version to the papers but unfortunately her chain wasn't long enough to reach the phone box. She died tragically in 1937 when Mrs Felicity Solicitor crashed into her while attempting to dial Directory Enquiries. As a mark of respect Mrs Solicitor vowed never to use her mobile phone again.

Mexico's president Juan Gonzales celebrates his 14th successive victory in his country's General Elections. He has been president since 1648.

In the sphere of domestic politics Stanley Baldwin, the Prime Minister, stunned the electorate when he announced plans for a new tax on hats (**below**). At public meetings throughout the country people were astonished by the news that trilbys, homburgs and cloth caps were soon to be subject to H.A.T. The ini-

tials H.A.T. stood for Headgear and Turbans. Baldwin was adamant that the tax should also encompass ethnic minorities. There was a predictable outcry from hat makers throughout the land who rightly saw this new tax as a threat to their businesses. The Amalgamated Milliners of Great Britain launched a massive advertising campaign to persuade people to stick with hats. Billboards throughout the land were soon covered in slogans proclaiming the value of headgear. *"Stick a hat on your head"* was perhaps not particularly inspired but many felt it was better than the long winded *"You might as well wear a hat because if you're late for work in the morning you don't have to waste time combing your hair before you leave the house."* This slogan backfired when the Amalgamated Hairbrush Manufacturers complained that it unfairly attacked their product and unless they received an apology they would have no alternative but to take industrial action. Futhermore, they were quite prepared to drag the hairdressers into the dispute as well. The Milliners refused to apologise and before long Britain

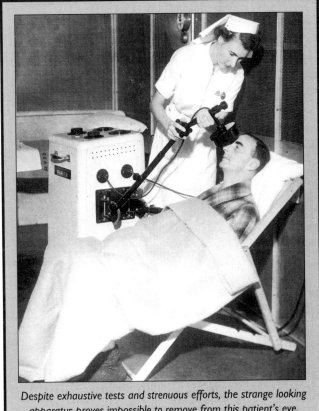

Despite exhaustive tests and strenuous efforts, the strange looking apparatus proves impossible to remove from this patient's eye.

was in the grip of an all-out barber strike. After three weeks of deadlock the government intervened by ordering senior civil servants to cut people's hair and by training parrots to help them out. A spokesman explained that, "Parrots are constantly grooming themselves so they should be able to offer expert advice. Also they work for nothing."

The chairman of the Amalgamated Milliners of Great Britain was Sir Hubert Tube; the very same man who had once been chairman of the "Bring Back The 19th

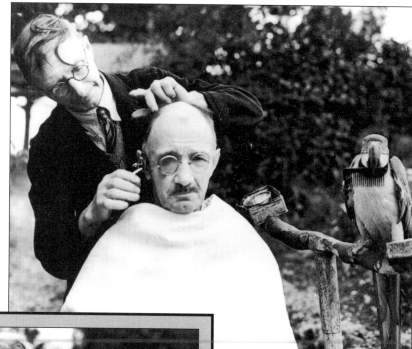

By using body odour alone the future Queen demonstrates how to stun a corgi.

Century Society". In the intervening years he had become a much respected businessman and had even been knighted in 1931 for services to stupidity. He was so incensed by Baldwin's proposed hat tax that he secretly engaged a shady desperado by the name of George Dull to follow the Prime Minister and to report on his movements in an attempt to accumulate information scandalous enough to bring down the Government. Dull was a master of disguise and he was proud of his ability to blend into any background. Studies of original photographs from the period using the very latest computer technology have identified Mr Dull for the very first time. In the photo **below** you may just be able

National Thumb Day proves as popular as ever.

to spot Dull disguised as a one-legged sea-dog. For the less observant amongst

you he is to the left of the Prime Minister. He's in workman guise **above** but again Baldwin is completely unaware of his presence. Dull takes a chance **below** by visually demonstrating his views on the hat tax but Baldwin (*arrowed*) is again blissfully unconcerned as he goes about his business.

The rather charming portrait on the **right** illustrates Dull's extraordinary ability to change his appearance at will. At first it was thought that our man had simply transformed himself into a rather obvious old woman, but a closer study reveals that Dull had, in fact, disguised himself as the pile of horse dung in the right hand corner of the photograph. Dull seemed to be untouchable until the police were given an anonymous tip off that a known criminal was swimming in the Thames disguised as a fish. At first the police doubted the information. A spokesman said, "The last place you would find a fish is in the Thames," but nevertheless the police felt duty bound to investigate (**below**). They found no trace of Dull. He was eventually captured while masquerading as a turkey

(**left**) and one of the most illustrious careers in 20th century criminology was brought to an end when he was eaten by several Chief Constables at the annual Metropolitan Police Christmas Party.

While the hat tax controversy dominated people's thoughts in this country, seasoned observers of foreign affairs were frightfully worried about what was happening in Nazi Germany.

In 1936 Hitler had used the Olympic Games as a propaganda platform for his vile politics. In a deeply cynical move he took people's innate love of pointing and transformed it into something evil. Suddenly the sport of pointing took on a whole new sinister aspect. On the **right** we see the German champion Konrad Heickle demonstrating the rather difficult outstretched leg point but the attitude is completely different from the poses adopted in the carefree 1900s. Here the athlete seems to be saying, "I'm going to point and there's damn all you can do about it." It was at these games that Hitler finally arrived at what he liked to call "the five-fingered point" (**below**). The rest of the world quickly dubbed it "the Nazi salute." Europe stumbled inevitably towards war in the late 1930s and when it was finally declared in September 1939 the hat tax was quietly and quickly dropped.

The Swedish men's synchronised pointing squad executing a delightful downward thrust with sidestep and toupé grip.

Herr Eric Jennings (background) looks on in disgust as Hitler walks off with his missus.

The 1940s:
War and Peace

By 1940, a year into the second world war, it was clear that the British Prime Minister, Neville Chamberlain, had to resign. His eyesight was rapidly failing and the Post Office was sick and tired of constantly enlarging his private correspondence (**right**). An interesting point, often overlooked by other historians, is that the piece of paper so proudly waved by Chamberlain upon his return from Munich in 1938 (**below**) did not in fact contain any promises of "peace in our time." It was actually a promotional leaflet for Grubers Second-Hand Doughnut Shop, a small take-away business often frequented by high-ranking Nazis.

Once Chamberlain had resigned, Parliament quickly agreed that Winston Churchill should be his replacement.

In an emotional speech Duncan Biscuits, the Conservative M.P. for Bridlington, told a packed House of Commons, "Churchill is exactly what this country needs in its darkest hour. A fat, bald alcoholic." Huge cheers greeted the remark and Churchill himself acknowledged the reaction by attempting to stand up. It was clear that, whereas Chamberlain had been a fairly non-descript politician, his successor was a larger-than-life individual. It was felt that this made him an easier target for Nazi assassins and that some kind of elaborate security plan would have to be developed. The first rather ludicrous idea was to disguise Churchill as a robot (**right**). This was felt to be impractical and the idea was abandoned. A life-size waxwork dummy was specially commissioned from Madame Tussaud's (**below**) but as the dummy was only capable of standing still with its eyes shut it

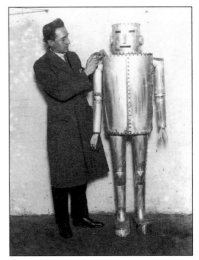

Nazi storm troopers arresting Herr Ludo Glockenspiel for illegally keeping two budgies in his mouth.

was felt to be too indistinguishable from the real thing. In a recently unearthed memo to the War Cabinet dated November 16th, 1940 the head of the security services, Sir Freeman Hardy-Willis wrote, *"The dummy is too lifelike and would cause endless confusion. We had returned the dummy to Madame Tussaud's where it was placed on display for over a week before we realised that we had actually returned the Prime Minister. The fact that the waxwork likeness was more effective in Cabinet is neither here nor there."* Certainly, by the end of 1940 some of Churchill's colleagues were disappointed by his lacklustre performance but close family friends attributed this to nerves and vodka.

In Nazi Germany, Adolf Hitler was showing early signs of the madness that one day would completely engulf him. In March 1941 he demanded that every house built in 1940 should be immediately demolished except for the living-room fireplace. Once the site had been cleared of all rubble Hitler himself would personally supervise the bricking-up of the remaining fireplace by qualified builders (**right**). Throughout 1941 some 17,000 fireplaces were bricked up in this manner. The firm that carried out this work, "Third Reich Builders,"

were at a loss as to why their beloved Führer would wish to brick up so many fireplaces but were perfectly happy merely to follow orders.

By 1942, Churchill had endeared himself to the British public with a series of publicity stunts specifically designed to endear himself to the British public. His famous "Wear a pointy hat and I'll give you tuppence" offer was quickly taken up by a population suffering severe hardship in the war-torn years. The amusing study **above** shows three little girls form the East End of London examining the luggage labels they had bought with their Churchill tuppences.

Britain, of course, was suffering all kinds of deprivation in the early 1940s. For a long while we stood alone against the might of the Nazi forces and Churchill tried many times to persuade America to enter the War, but naturally enough, the U.S.A. was reluctant to join the fighting until they could be sure which side was winning.

The hardship that Britain suffered in these war years manifested itself in several ways. By 1944 there seemed to be a chronic shortage of everything. Lack of available manpower meant that London's transport system was taken over by

"Haben Sie wirklich nur ein bal, mein Führer?"

Churchill addressing two lucky soldiers: "Now don't spend it all at once."

An unexploded toddler being removed from the beach at Margate.

Whipsnade Zoo. Ostrich taxis (**above**) were soon seen plying their trade up and down Regent Street. The Animal Transport Scheme, as it was officially called, fell into disrepute however when a six foot white rabbit called Gary got

hopelessly pissed one night and refused to take a fare to Piccadilly Circus. The passenger, a Mr Pillbeam, was quoted in the national press as saying, *"It's a lark innit"*. When a rather pedantic passer-by told Pillbeam that it was in fact a *rabbit* he was punched in the spleen. The final nail in the coffin for the Animal Transport Scheme was a bizarre incident that happened in the Summer of 1944. A prehistoric dragon, previously thought extinct, was rather recklessly put in charge of inspecting passengers' tickets on the Bakerloo Line. Predictably, it ran amok when it caught its tail in the down escalator at Wembley Central. For

three days and three nights it stomped around the capital causing untold damage; particularly in the East End of London. This damage was later officially blamed on "Bombs dropped by the Luftwaffa." The Government was so embarrassed by the dragon running amok that even today official spokesmen deny that it ever happened. The dragon was eventually killed by five plucky firemen who managed to drown it by holding its head down in a bucket of cold water. Although the Animal Transport Scheme was officially discredited by the end of 1944, it had nevertheless struck a chord in the imagi-

War Office strategists trying to find somewhere safe for their summer holidays.

nation of the public. In India, which at that time was still of course part of the Great British Empire, many adventurous young men decided to kiss alligators (**below**). They reasoned that if ostriches could drive taxis there was no reason

In an attempt to pay for the enormous cost of the war effort, Hitler visits a betting shop to try and pick the winner of the 1943 Grand National.

why alligators wouldn't make perfectly acceptable sexual partners. The logic may be rather difficult to follow, but their obvious dedication to the task in hand quickly dispelled any criticisms that they were just a bunch of nutters mucking around in a sand-pit.

By the middle of 1945, the Second World War was over. Nazi Germany had been defeated by the allies, and Japan surrendered after America dropped the world's first atomic bomb on Hiroshima. Suddenly the world was confronted with the reality of weapons capable of mass destruction. Amongst the countless victims of Hiroshima was Mr Pillbeam who, only a year earlier, had suffered the indignity of sitting in the back of a taxi while a six foot rabbit called Gary sang *The Sun Has Got His Hat On* in a drunken slur. Rather unluckily for him, Mr Pillbeam arrived in Hiroshima just two hours before the bomb. He checked into his hotel, then crossed over the road for a paper and got run down by a bus. A tragic story amongst millions.

And so peace was finally declared. People celebrated in many different ways. The Duchess of Argyll (**opposite**) scandalised polite society by smoking a huge

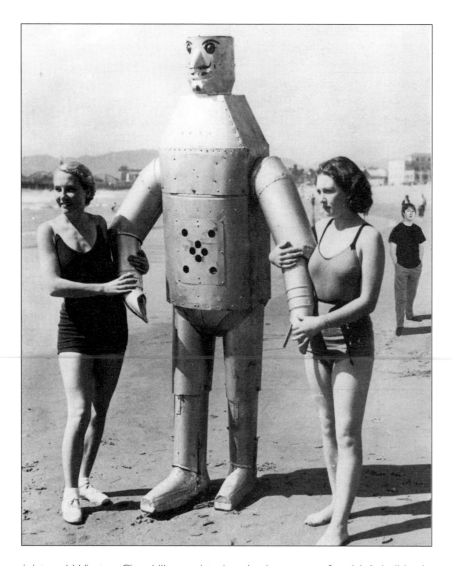

joint and Winston Churchill, our victorious leader, spent a fortnight's holiday in Skegness disguised as a robot (**above**). The British people would never forget Churchill's outstanding leadership but they still felt that it was time for a change. Labour won a massive majority in the 1945 General Election and a hitherto unnoticed politician called Clement Attlee found himself as the new Prime Minister. In an emotional speech to the House of Commons, Duncan Biscuits, the Conservative M.P. for Bridlington, said, "Who's Clement Attlee?" Huge cheers greeted this remark and Atlee himself acknowledged the reaction by pretending to be somebody called Bert Drainpipe.

The new governing party introduced a dazzling collection of reforms and new ideas. Perhaps their finest achievement was the introduction of the National Health Service specifically designed to meet the medical needs of those people less able to afford hospital treatment. There are unsubstantiated rumours that this service still exists even today.

By the end of the 1940s there was an air of quiet optimism about. People believed for the first time that good times were just around the corner.

The 1950s:
Rock and Roll Years

In many respects the 1950s were aptly named. To foster the belief that good times really were just around the corner the government announced that a Festival of Britain would be held on the South Bank of the Thames. The public were invited to marvel at some of the wonderful new design ideas that would surely re-confirm Britain's status as a major innovative world power. Amongst the innovations on display was the newly designed non-transparent window (**right**).

The official Festival programme described it in the following manner. *"The non-transparent window is a major breakthrough in contemporary design. Instead of utilising traditional glass the window is entirely constructed from brickwork. This means that several can be installed into an ordinary brick wall without changing its appearance in any*

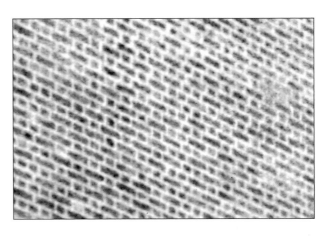

Heidi Glockenspiel carrying on the family tradition.

way. What's more, these new windows never need cleaning and are maintenance free." The British public, recognising a good idea when they didn't see one, immediately bought these revolutionary windows in their thousands. Throughout the Summer of 1951 the sound of bricks being knocked out of walls and replaced with other bricks echoed up and down the land.

Although Britain was totally confident of its status in the international arena the other World Powers were not so sure. During an otherwise routine meeting of the United Nations Security Council the Russian representative suddenly turned to his British counterpart and said, "You're a man of the world, nip out and buy us twenty fags will you?" This calculated insult led the British representative, Sir Geoffrey Uck-Witt, to immediately demand that the other nations censure the Russian for his overtly patronising manner. An emergency meeting was called and after some deliberation Uck-Witt was summoned to the General Secretary's office. Here he was told – and I quote

Disaster strikes at the Queen's coronation when, during final rehearsals somebody breaks in and steals all the people.

from the official records, *"And while your about it get a pint of milk as well."*

George VI maintained Royal tradition by dying in 1952 and when his successor Elizabeth II was crowned the following year, millions of people were able to watch the Coronation on their newly purchased television sets. These early sets were a far cry from their modern technological counterparts. Although extremely bulky the actual screen size was no bigger than an ant's lung (**below**).

BBC radio which at this time enjoyed its highest ever listening figures was understandably anxious about this new competitor. Top secret talks were held in a top secret location, but because everything was so top secret it's impossible to tell if these top secret talks related in any way to anything in particular. Chances are they probably did. Or not as the case may be.

Undoubtedly the biggest radio star of the 1950s was

the all-round entertainer Billy "Where's my teeth?" Moncur (**above**). Millions adored his light-hearted banter, although in retrospect his style is a little corny. Here is a typical extract from one of his many radio shows.

DOOR OPENS:

MRS FOOTBALL:

How are you today, Billy? Bright and cheerful I'll be bound.

BILLY: I want to die.

MRS FOOTBALL:

How about a nice cuppa? That'll cheer you up.

BILLY: Leave me alone or I'll kill you.

MRS FOOTBALL:

Oh, things can't be that bad. After all . . . stop it Billy, your hurting me . . . I can't breath . . . Billy . . . I . . . Arrggh!

P.C. William Horse can't figure out what is going on here and neither can I.

A little known fact about Elvis Presley (11½ stone) was that he could completely remove his head and roll it from one hand to the other along his shoulders.

In its day this was considered laugh-a-minute stuff. Unfortunately, Billy Moncur found fame very difficult to deal with and always disliked being recognised in the street. While being interviewed by *Pathé Newsreel* he was approached by a well wisher who courteously requested his autograph. The following is a transcribe of the dialogue from the original newsreel soundtrack:

WELL WISHER: Mr Moncur, could I trouble you for an autograph? Mr Moncur . . . I can't breathe . . . please . . . I . . . Arrggh!

Billy Moncur murdered eighty-seven people throughout the 1950s. Although often arrested he was never actually charged. As one policeman at the time said, "He's such a cheeky chappy you can't help overlooking the carnage."

Billy eventually received his come-uppance when he was punched in the face by an off-duty wrestler in an all night dry cleaners off the Old Kent Road. His tortured cries of "Where's my teeth" merely convinced onlookers that he was rehearsing a new sketch for his radio show.

The Great Hugo, circus performer, refused to tame any lion until he had been formally introduced.

In 1956 the nation's youth were suddenly gripped by Rock and Roll. A new word was invented; teenagers. And teenagers had money and they knew how to spend it. Dance halls all over the country were soon rocking and rolling to this infectious new music. Even Siamese twins had a whale of a time (**right**). By the end of the decade Elvis Presely had established himself as the King of Rock and Roll and he weighed 11½ stone.

By the middle of the '50s it seemed that Britain at last was finding its feet. Rationing finally disappeared in 1954 and to convince the public that prosperity was within the country's grasp, every neighbourhood community in the South-east of England was given its very own robot (**below**). In a party political broadcast a Government spokesman explained, "Now that the shops are once again full of produce busy housewives may experience difficulty in finding the time to sort through all the various goods on display. This irksome task can be safely entrusted to robots who are programmed to buy all the essential groceries while Mother puts her feet up for a well-earned rest." Unfortunately, the robots were near useless. Because of their extremely slow walking pace it took them ages to complete the simplest of tasks.

After several weeks absence many housewives were understandably distressed by the robots' sudden re-appearance at their kitchen door, carrying a basket full of congealed groceries. The public dissatisfaction with the robots soon

led to them being nicknamed Geoffrey after Sir Geoffrey Uck-Witt, the man so comprehensively humiliated after being forced to go shopping for the Security Council of the United Nations. The scheme fell into total disrepute when it was revealed that the robot serving Arbitration Street in Bromley was actually Winston Churchill up to his old tricks again.

In the area of physical endeavour, however, there was much to cheer. On June 1st, 1953 Edmund Hillary and Sherpa Tensing became the first men to stand on the summit of Mount Everest. Hillary's much reported remark, "No man can stand higher and still remain on Earth" provoked the British adventurer Peter Sout to climb Everest the following year with a stepladder under his arm (**right**). As Sout stood at the top of the stepladder on

To improve his ability to leap above defenders, Chelsea's brilliant young forward Jimmy Greaves is encouraged to eat grass on the basis that cows can jump over the moon.

the peak of the world's highest mountain news reached him that Roger Bannister has just run the world's first ever sub-four minute mile. Bannister's claim that, "No man has ever before covered such a distance in such a time without the aid of mechanical contraptions" so enraged Sout that he immediately attempted to beat the record by throwing himself off the north face of the mountain. On his way down he was heard to shout to a group of bemused sherpas "Look, I've already done four hundred yards in 8.4 seconds." He continued to fall past them and disappeared into a huge snow-covered ravine.

His obituary printed in *The Daily Telegraph* a few days later rightly paid tribute to *"his bravery and, above all, his stupidity."*

Frank Sinatra knits himself a woman.

Towards the end of the decade it was clear that both the Russians and the Americans were spending millions in a race to put the first man on the moon. Sir Geoffrey Uck-Witt was admonished by the Prime Minister for not finding out about it sooner. Sir Geoffrey's defence that whenever the Americans were discussing this kind of thing he was inevitably out buying bin liners for the Chinese did not go down very well.

Ingrid Bergman is accosted in Rome by a 25-foot tall flasher

Conservative party candidate Margaret Roberts (Thatcher to be) was confident of a local election victory in the certain knowledge that the labour candidate would mysteriously retire.

To test the potentially harmful effects of space travel, the Americans strapped a tiny monkey into a specially re-designed hot water bottle (**left**), placed it inside a small rocket and then blasted it fifty-five miles into outer space. When asked by the world's press why a monkey had been chosen for this dangerous experiment, the scientist in charge of the operation, Professor Sam Irwin, replied, "I don't like little monkeys."

By 1959 it was clear that once again the world had changed far more rapidly than most people could cope with. But those people who felt dizzy after a decade of radical change were in for a bit of a shock. The '60s were just around the corner.

Margaret Roberts helpfully indicates to the unfortunate Labour Party candidate the exact location of his testicles.

The 1960s:
Love and Peace

The decade began slowly. March 4th was a particularly slow day. April 17th wasn't much better and July 9th positively dawdled along. People were aware however that there was a questioning mood in the air. The problem was that nobody was quite sure what the actual question might be. It soon emerged that there were two conflicting schools of thought. The eminent philosopher Henry Tomorrow suggested the question was "Is God dead?", but a London taxi driver called Edgar Weedon thought the question was more likely

As The Beatles arrive back from Australia, Captain Cliff Duran egotistically wonders why everybody wants to take his photo.

to be "Have you got change for a fiver?" The popular newspaper of the day, the *Daily Liar*, attempted to resolve the conflict by sponsoring a series of philosophical discussions at the Royal Albert Hall. These were widely advertised as *"The Egghead versus the Cabby"* debates. Throughout the long argumentative sessions the two sides remained unmovable. Tomorrow claimed that God must be dead because there was no philosophical basis for maintaining his existence, while Weedon took the view that although he often did have change for a fiver he couldn't always guarantee it.

The questioning mood hanging over Britain was further fuelled in 1961 when four Oxbridge graduates staged a show at the Edinburgh Festival called *Beyond The Fringe*. Theatre-goers were shocked by Peter Cook's portrayal of the then Prime Minister, Harold Macmillan. This was the first time that such a prominent politician had been lampooned on stage. Distressed audience members was given individual oxygen cylinders to help them survive the performance. Peter Cook later recalled that, whenever he was on particularly good form, "You could hear frantic sucking from the first three rows." Before *Beyond The Fringe* other performers had attempted to impersonate the Prime Minister but had always lacked the courage to use his proper name. In 1959 Billy "Where's my teeth" Moncur had starred in an ill-fated revue called *Don't Go, It Gets Better* in

Prince Charles officially becomes the first man in Britain to have his hair designed by Dulux paints.

In a Vatican sponsored exercise, Carmelite nuns smoke marijuana.

Within days the effects are obvious.

The world's first brain transplant is considered a dismal failure when the patient sneezes and the new brain shoots out of his nose.

which he portrayed a character called Barold Bacmillan and the noted character actor Jocelyn Crowds had enjoyed a huge personal success with his one man show *"Sarold Sucmillan – Man of Destiny"*.

Beyond The Fringe attacked politicians, religion, World War Two and in one misguided sketch, central heating. The show success led to the publication of a satirical magazine called *Private Eye* and the broadcast of a television series called *That Was The Week That Was*. The satire boom was underway and society's sacred cows were held up to intense ridicule. Bob Dylan recorded a song called *The Times They Are A' Changing* and a lot of people sighed and said "Oh no not again."

In June 1963 the British establishment was rocked to its very foundations when John Profumo, the Secretary of State for War, told the House of Commons that he'd once had sex with a polar bear. Amidst shouts of "Resign" and "What was it like?", Profumo left public office with as much dignity as he could muster. Harold Macmillan attempted to restore confidence to the Conservative ranks by pointing out that, although the country seemed to be in a temporary state of turmoil, at least crime was being tackled head on. Two weeks later, the Great Train Robbery happened. A gang of masked men stole the London to Glasgow express and refused to give it back until there was a fifteen per cent reduction in the cost of an annual season ticket. Having made a fool of himself Macmillan appeared on live television and declared "that although we have our troubles we must take our lead from the United States of America. Their charismatic President is a very popular man and will lead the West into an age of unrivalled prosperity. Even as I speak he is enjoying a drive around Dallas in an open

The State of Utah officially welcomes President Kennedy by showing him a fat bloke sitting on top of a horse that badly needs a haircut.

Not only did peace and love become part of the political agenda but sales of eye-shadow quadrupled.

topped car, waving to his supporters and enjoying their natural good humour."

At this point in his speech the Prime Minister was interrupted by a frantic aide who handed him a piece of paper. The P.M. read with horror that President Kennedy had just been assassinated in Dallas. Not wishing to appear a complete mug he pretended that he'd just been handed the football results. The nation watched agog as Macmillan, fighting back the tears, declared "Southampton 1 – Fulham 2". Bemused viewers could

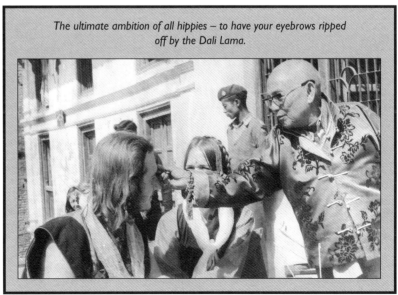

The ultimate ambition of all hippies – to have your eyebrows ripped off by the Dali Lama.

Mrs Kennedy has a bizarre premonition and indicates the exact point at which the first bullet will enter the President's brain.

only surmise that the Prime Minister was a somewhat sensitive Southampton supporter.

The following day everybody knew the truth. Or did they? At the time it was widely believed that Lee Harvey Oswald had shot the President from an open window as the motorcade drove past. But evidence collected over the years has thrown doubt over that judgement. I have investigated the matter myself and I have often been puzzled as to why nobody has seen fit to try and get President Kennedy's own view of his death. Despite constant applications to interview the dead man I was continually fobbed off with the excuse that it was inconvenient to talk to the President because he had a bit of a headache.

Oswald, who was arrested a few hours after the killing, maintained his innocence throughout the last two days of his life. He told police "I remembered the stories that my Grandfather used to tell me about the days when people loved to point. It sounded kinda fun and so I thought I would point at the President as he drove past. Admittedly I was pointing with an automatic weapon but what's

The Ku Klux Klan hold their annual beauty contest.

wrong with that?" Within a few hours of being charged Oswald was gunned down by nightclub owner Jack Ruby. Ruby himself was killed two weeks later by an unemployed blacksmith called Jim Sweeney, who was in turn murdered the following day by a part-time female impressionist called Mary Kinnie. Three days later, Kinnie was fatally killed by a drunk driver identified by the police as Alice Vranch. Vranch was released on bail only to be crushed to death by a falling ostrich deliberately dropped from a 14th storey window by a drunken construction worker named Joe Lawrence. Lawrence then tripped over a rope and fell to his death. He landed on the ostrich which still had a tiny bit of

Harold Wilson was not only the Labour Prime Minister, he was also Britain's Champion Pet-Hurler. Here we see him about to hurl a labrador 235 yards.

The Prime Minister's wife says goodbye to her cat as her husband, with a deft flick of his wrist, propels the luckless animal into a suburban back garden three streets away.

biscuit stuck in its throat from a previous meal. The biscuit shot out of the ostrich's mouth and struck a passer-by in the heart, instantly killing him. The

passer-by, a Mr Cranston Mullarky, fell into the path of a luxury coach, owned by Simpson Tours, which ploughed into an orphanage killing everybody on board. This series of deaths further convinced sceptics that some kind of cover-up was going on.

Back home Labour won a General Election and as an editorial in *The Guardian* put it *"Well, if the times are a' changing, let's get on with it."*

By the mid-sixties Rock and Roll had become Rock. Rock was considered to be much more than just dance music. Fanatics were listening to their favourite records in an attempt to gain some kind of mystical insight into the workings of the Universe. This search was often fuelled by the con-sumption of such mind-altering drugs as

The Beverly Brothers, three notorious pigeon stranglers, attempt to hide the evidence during an identity parade. Notice that the pigeon on the left appears to be smoking a cigarette.

L.S.D. One American devotee of the Beatles claimed that the secret of life would be revealed if you played *Eleanor Rigby* backwards. The fan Randy Treesucker claimed you could hear John Lennon repeating the same phrase over

'Table service is undoubtedly slow in some European cafes' claims top level EEC report.

and over again. Although Treesucker had written the words down they still didn't make any sense to him. The phrase was *"Have you got change of a fiver?"*

Flower power blossomed in 1967 and the youth of the world were urged to go to San Francisco. The Mayor of San Francisco was forced to issue a statement asking everybody not to turn up at once otherwise there would be a hell of a queue for the public conveniences.

The Woodstock openair festival was held and the air was filled with

The Beatles hold a press conference to deny allegations of drug-taking but their denials are not taken seriously because they enter the room at an approximate height of thirty-five feet.

the spirit of free love. Musicians became gods and Paul McCartney further infuriated the already extremely jittery establishment when he admitted in a newspaper interview that *"Yes, I do have change for a fiver."*

Harold Macmillan was brought out by the old guard to try and convince young people not to turn their back on traditional values. In an emotional party political broadcast he told the nation, "It may seem to you all that the world has turned upside down. But hey, it's cool. Things haven't really changed, man. It's not as if anybody has landed on the moon." Two days later,

The Prime Minister follows the trajectory of a recently chucked chihuahua.

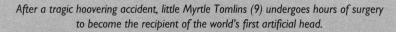

After a tragic hoovering accident, little Myrtle Tomlins (9) undergoes hours of surgery to become the recipient of the world's first artificial head.

In the 1990s this man suddenly came from out of nowhere to make no impact whatsoever. Here he is in 1969 doing much the same thing.

man landed on the moon. That night the citizens of the world looked skyward. The moon looked the same but mankind had surely changed. Perhaps world peace was a possibility after all. Clear photographs of the earth were transmitted back to the earth. For the first time in the history of the world human beings could look at the world and say "That's where we live. That's where we all live."

Macmillan wasted no time in telling the press that he was firmly convinced that "War was over. And in future Man will live in perfect harmony." He was wrong, again.

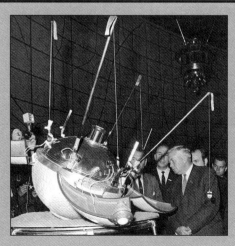

Harold Wilson is suitably humbled as he receives the British All Champion Pet Hurlers Trophy for the third successive year.

The 1970s:
Punk Politics

The euphoric mood engendered by the late 1960s was quickly dissipated when it was soon realised that the only tangible result of the previous decade was that young people were walking around in stupid looking clothes. Ridiculously flared trousers and paisley shirts with unfeasibly long collars were everywhere and so the establishment breathed a sigh of relief. They reasoned that if they younger generation couldn't even get their fashion sense right then a bloody revolution was highly unlikely.

The Conservatives won the General Election in 1970 with a campaign that heavily criticised the Labour party. The Tory party's slogan *"DON'T VOTE FOR LABOUR – THEY'RE A BUNCH OF RUDDY NUTTERS"* was applauded in media

Florida scientist invents dental floss for killer whales.

Human beings mutate while trying to get through to directory enquiries.

circles as a breath of fresh air. The R.S.P.R.N (The Royal Society for the Protection of Ruddy Nutters – Patron Prince Philip) protested that politicians should not be described as "Ruddy Nutters" because this was demeaning to "Ruddy Nutters". The Society was dismissed by the media as "Ruddy Nutters".

In 1973, the Prime Minister, Edward Teeth ran into serious political trouble when a protracted Miners Strike led to the introduction of a three day week. Britain was running out of electricity and so in order to conserve as much as possible, Tuesdays, Thursdays, Saturdays and Mondays were temporarily removed from the calendar. This move provoked uproar. With more than half of the traditional week disappearing overnight people suddenly found themselves getting older much quicker. Fifty-two weeks per annum meant that a year only lasted one hundred and fifty-six days. Caroline Amanda Jane Jones, a spokeswoman for the newly

Mrs Eileen Jacobs hypnotises the entire cabinet with her plump arms.

Cilla Black makes a comeback.

formed "7 Day Club", articulated the fears of many when she told the *Daily Useless*, in an exclusive interview, *"If the three day week continues everybody in twenty years' time will be forty years older. Who is going to look after all those geriatrics?"* Sensing that he was onto a loser Teeth backtracked and suggested that the missing four days could be reinstated providing that the traditional sixty minutes in an hour were reduced to thirty. Minutes would thus become thirty seconds long. This piece of sharp political manoeuvring was quickly nipped in the bud by the "7 Days Club" who wasted no time in highlighting the absurdities of the idea. As Miss Jones pointed out "A three minute egg will be inedible if its only boiled for ninety seconds. And it normally takes me twenty minutes to travel to work, I can't possibly be expected to make the same journey in ten."

The Royal Family watch as Princess Margaret's gin supply is airlifted in by the R.A.F.

Although the three day week dominated thoughts at home, America was about to be engulfed in its biggest political crisis since the Second World War – Watergate. After a long and exhaustive inquiry President Richard Nixon was found guilty of making faces behind senior politicians when he thought nobody was looking. Nixon resigned and was replaced by Gerald Ford, perhaps the most inept politician ever to hold high office. Among his more ludicrous public declarations he claimed that there was no Soviet domination of Eastern Europe and that chocolate was capable of intelligent thought.

In an extraordinary broadcast to the American people the President appeared with a large Easter egg which he introduced as Roy (**below**). After a few words he placed the microphone in front of the chocolate egg and invited it to address the nation. Roy's speech was rather difficult to understand as it was clear that the President was attempting to speak for Roy by placing his hand over his own mouth. It has been suggested that Ford stole this idea from President Roosevelt who, in 1930, had boosted American morale with a celebrated series of fireside chats. These radio broadcasts, in which Roosevelt pretended to chat

Keith Richards is arrested for drug abuse after he fails a cake cutting test.

to his fireside, were tremendously popular and one exchange in particular became famous throughout the United States:

ROOSESVELT: Tell me, do you like being a fireside?

FIRESIDE: Sure. It's better than being a communist.

Ford's re-introduction of this stylistic device seriously backfired on him when opinion polls revealed that on the whole the American people would rather be governed by Roy.

Here Mrs Thatcher is clearly thinking *"I know something you don't know."*

Back home the government attempted to regain the voters' confidence by publicly demonstrating the effects of a new bomb developed by British scientists. This recent invention was hailed in some quarters as a positive addition to the British defence programme. The bomb was unique in that while it totally vaporised human beings it left their wellington boots intact. Despite serious objections it was tested on a group of farmers who were tricked into standing together on the pretext that they were attempting to beat the world record for the number of farmers standing together in a relatively small area (**above**).

Labour won the general election and Edward Teeth was replaced as Tory leader by Margaret Thatcher. Mrs Thatcher wasted no time in stamping her personality on British politics. Within two weeks of becoming Leader of the

Lord Hailsham is taken for a walk in the park.

Opposition she introduced her exceedingly popular "What is Crap?" campaign (**above**). The campaign consisted of Mrs Thatcher touring the country and asking small groups of people the simple question, "What is Crap?" If the

answers were, "The Labour Party" or, "Britain under a Labour administration", Mrs Thatcher would present them with a specially printed "What is Crap?" poster and wish them the very best of luck for the future. The campaign quickly seized the public's imagination and soon Britain's inventors, who had been fairly quiet for some time, were competing for the "crappiest invention that anybody could think of " award. The undisputed winner was Tommy De Lauren who took it into his head to invent a caravan stuck onto a hovercraft (**right**).

While Mrs Thatcher was whipping up support for her party the Labour Prime Minister James Callaghan was beset by a string of industrial disputes. Upon re-

gaining power Labour had abolished the much hated three day week and had granted the miners their much delayed wage increase. However, other sections of society demanded their slice of the cake as well, In early 1976 Britain's clowns took industrial action and soon began to create havoc with a highly organised campaign designed to bring the country to its knees. Clowns in charge of school skiing trips (**below**) would suddenly surprise the children by whacking one of them over the head with a wickerwork picnic basket. Comedians were soon dragged into the dispute as well. Comics all over the country suddenly refused to be funny. Jim Bowen spoke for many of his fellow performers when he said, "I now go on stage

Bobo demands a 15% pay increase.

determined to be unfunny. And I shall continue to do so until the clowns receive their well deserved pay rise." Unfortunately for Mr Bowen the dispute lasted for nearly twenty years but he was nevertheless as good as his word.

By early 1977 those people who were still wearing flared trousers and paisley shirts were outraged by the emergence of a new raw music called Punk. Overnight, rock's elder statesmen were described as dinosaurs and

The reason why the Sex Pistols were formed.

The reason why the Bay City Rollers disbanded.

the Sex Pistols became the most popular beat combo around. As if to confirm that the old music had gone forever, Elvis Presley died at the absurdly young age of 42. He weighed 35 stone. Soon the Sex Pistols were embroiled in scandal when it was erroneously disclosed that they didn't actually play on any of their records. Soon rumours circulated that they were even miming at their own press conferences.

In one interview with the *Melody Maker*, Johnny Rotten stunned a journalist by replying to the question "Why are you a Punk?" with the words, "It's better than being a communist." The journalist immediately noticed something wrong. Not only did Mr Rotten's words fail to match his lip movements but they were also spoken in a deep American accent with the sound of a roaring fire somewhere in the distance. Malcolm McLaren, the group's manager, later claimed that Mr Rotten's strange behaviour was entirely due to the fact

Prime Minister Callaghan sees for himself that the Picadilly Line extension is still not complete.

The Conservative Party's 1922 Committee celebrates its 50th anniversary.

that he had a slight headache. The Pistols ran into further trouble when they released the single *"God Save The Queen"* during the height of Elizabeth II's jubilee celebrations. One particular couplet, *"God save the Queen, she ain't no human being"* caused outrage until the record company hastily issued a press statement claiming that the lyric had been misheard. According to them the actual word were *"God save the Queen, she ain't no haricot bean."* Nobody could argue with this and the matter was quickly forgotten.

By the end of the decade Punk had more or less blown itself out but its original emergence had clearly shown that once again the nation's youth were not willing to accept the previous generation's values. Peace and love had clearly failed and instead of waving flowers the kids were now brandishing chainsaws. Their behaviour frightened the more sedate elements in society and people were soon to be spotted hanging around street corners muttering, "What is the world coming to." Britain was not at ease with itself and it was desperately searching for a new direction; a leader who could unite the country and put the Great back into Britain. And so in June 1979 Mrs Margaret Thatcher became Prime Minister. Harold Macmillian immediately declared that she would be good for the country.

As soon as it hits the shops, Margaret Thatcher is first in line to buy an Edward Heath giant jigsaw puzzle

The 1980s:
Avarice and Snooker

It didn't take long for the 1980s to establish themselves as the eighties decade. Under Margaret Thatcher's leadership people were encouraged to believe that money was the root of all pleasure. "Yuppies" were identified for the first time and for those who had money the shops were full of new inventions. Compact discs and video recorders appeared and hi-fi television sets appealed to those people who wanted to watch rubbish in stereo. Keep fit videos were all the rage with the most popular being *"Shape Up and Dance With Pope John Paul."* Channel 4 began broadcasting in 1982 and quickly established itself as a home for comedians with fake cockney accents.

The following year Hitler's' alleged diaries were discovered. Although at first their discovery was hailed as the most remarkable historical find of the century, it soon became clear that they were in fact a rather crude forgery. Here is an extract:

Shape Up and Dance with Pope John Paul.

During a tennis quarter-final match, Martina Navratilova raises a much needed laugh by impersonating the man standing immediately behind her.

AUGUST 31ST: It was a lovely day so I went for a walk in the park. Met a very attractive bit of skirt and brought her home. At first her husband, Herr Eric Jennings, objected but once I told him that I was Hitler and I could do what I like he soon shut his row.

SEPTEMBER IST: Invaded Poland

The legendary Steve Davis who, throughout his career, managed to avoid playing the even more legendary Jack Milk.

The fastest growing sport in Britain in the 1980s was undoubtedly snooker. New sports heroes were created overnight. Steve Davis and Jimmy White became household names but the undoubted king of the green baize table was the legendary Jack Milk. His was an extraordinary story. Shipwrecked at

Lady Di demonstrates that the sun really does shine out of her backside.

an early age he was raised by a flock of seagulls on a remote tropical island two hundred miles off the coast of Barmy Land. He learnt a great deal from the seagulls as he later acknowledged. "Because of all the time that I spent with them I can distinguish 37 types of fish and I can also fly." Jack demonstrated his extraordinary ability during the 1983 finals when in the middle of a century break he suddenly flew around the table at a height of 15 feet before finally settling on top of a television camera. His opponent, Vic Spit, bitterly complained that Milk's flight around the room was designed to break his concentration. The referee, George Clueless, feared that he was going mad and totally denied that he had just seen a professional snooker player perform a loop the loop in mid-air. Realising that he couldn't expect justice from the officials Spit retaliated by having a heart

The Pope exhorts his followers to "Feel the Burn".

attack. Seeing that his opponent had outmanoeuvred him, Milk immediately struck back by lapsing into a deep coma. Spit now knew that he had a fight on his hands. He immediately upped the stakes by calling for a life support machine but no sooner was it wheeled into the arena than Milk requested the tournament priest to give him the last rites. Within seconds Spit declared himself officially dead and immediately demanded his own cremation. As the first gallon of petrol was poured over Spit, Milk announced that he had just died, as a matter of fact, and then had been miraculously re-incarnated as himself. Spit had no answer to this and watched morosely, in flames, as his opponent continued to clear the table. With such exciting matches as these it was no wonder that snooker became the most popular television sport of the decade. Of course not everybody was a snooker fan. Chief amongst the game's critics was Lionel Sod, then noted media commentator. He described the sport as "Simply being nothing more than old fashioned pointing with sticks. If the younger generation had

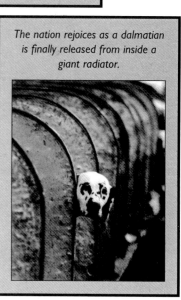

The nation rejoices as a dalmatian is finally released from inside a giant radiator.

any guts at all they would scrap the cues, the balls and the table and simply point for the sheer pleasure of it. "

In 1985 Orson Welles, one of Hollywood's few genuine talents, died. As has been remarked elsewhere his life's work seemed to run backwards. His career should really have started with beer commercials and ended with him producing

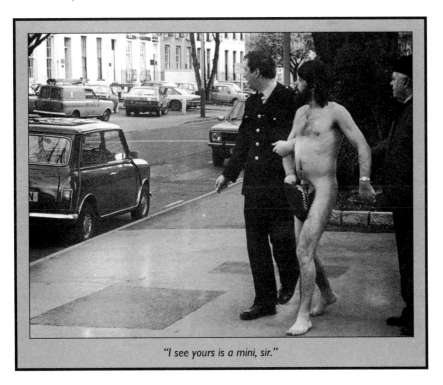

"I see yours is a mini, sir."

Richard Branson announces cheaper air fares.

the greatest film ever made. Orson Welles' self-proclaimed number one fan was a rather deranged Californian called Bucky Alfalfa. As soon as he heard about the death of his hero Bucky announced that, as his own personal tribute, he had decided to get very fat. Forcing himself to eat a diet that consisted entirely of foam rubber. Alfalfa's weight quickly ballooned to an extraordinary eighty-five stone. In his unpublished account, *"Don't Eat Foam Rubber"*, Bucky tells his own miserable story, *"It just got to the point where my behind was so large the only way I could walk was to sling a buttock over each shoulder and pretend I was carrying two very ugly babies. I got away with it for a long time and during election campaigns politicians used to kiss them!"*

In 1986, Harold Macmillan, the grand elder statesman of British politics, told the *Daily Fascist* that he had never felt better in his entire life. He of course died as soon as the interview was over.

In her most compassionate voice, Mrs Thatcher tells Harold MacMillan that she's going to put him in a home.

Pope John Paul gets a hernia while demonstrating an abdominal stretch.

The Titanic was rediscovered in 1985 and for the first time people could study underwater photographs of the wreckage. Amazingly a survivor was found on board. Her name was Elizabeth Bett-Noir (pictured **right**) and she told rescuers that she had been trapped in an air pocket since 1912. Once safely aboard the rescue ship Miss Bett-Noir eagerly demanded a full account of everything that had happened since the Titanic had sunk. "Do people still enjoy table sprawling?" she asked. The ship's crew, weary after a long day's diving, ignored her questions and locked her in a small cupboard with a bowl of minestrone soup. The next day she was handed an early draft of this same book that you are reading and was amazed to discover that not only had women got the vote but that a woman was also Prime Minister. She was outraged by the accounts of the First World War and when she asked why it was called the First World War she was directed to the section dealing with the Second. Appalled by this picture of global butchery she was then astonished to

During the 1988 Highland Games God drops a toothpick and Moray Docherty is the first to notice.

When Vincenzo Nicoli's bicycle is stolen in 1986 he immediately organises a posse.

read that man had landed on the moon. But even more astonishing was the fact Miss Bett-Noir was reading the account of her reading this book while she was relaxing in the captain's cabin reading this book. When she asked how this was possible, she was fobbed off with the lame excuse that it was just a writer's trick. As the rescue ship sailed home Miss Bett-Noir was encouraged to try her hand at shark fishing. After a couple of days she delighted the crew by catching a hammer-head shark off the coast of Brazil. To everybody's complete bewilderment, when the shark's belly was ripped open, a small black and white photograph of a female athlete was found nestling next to the spleen. It was of course a photo of Fran Potterton, the noted Canadian pointer. Readers with fairly well developed long term memories will remember that this picture was first referred to in Chapter One. Throughout a long after-noon everybody racked their brains for a possible solution to this extraordinary occurrence before finally settling on the thought that these things happen.

In the world of domestic politics Mrs Thatcher won her third election victory in a row and later that same year England suffered its worst storm of the century. Some Labour politicians claimed that it was God's judgement on Thatcherite policies but Mrs Thatcher assured them that she had nothing to do with it. The sight of trees lying in the streets prompted

Elton John models Watford's new away strip.

Margaret Thatcher spearheads a search for Roy's immediate family.

Mrs Mary Stupid (**above**) to phone her local radio station and told a bemused disc jockey that it was just like World War Two. "Oh really" said the D.J., with heavy irony. "I had no idea that the Germans had been dropping branches all over London. I can see it now – 'Mr Churchill come quickly, there's an oak tree in Trafalgar Square... and it's not one of ours.' And then Churchill in that wonderful delivery of his simply replied, 'Wait till the conker season arrives and then we'll show them.'" This apparently banal exchange is

Pope John Paul's meeting with President Giscard D'Estang is considered a failure when it transpires that both men are too shy to face each other.

actually of great interest to us historians. It marks the first recorded utterances of Mrs Mary Stupid who was to play an absolutely crucial role in the history of the 20th Century.

And so the decade finished more or less as it had begun. With a year with a one and nine and an eight in it. Youth's brief fling with love and peace in the 1960s became Punk's anarchy in the 1970s. And the youth of the 1980s were by and large motivated by greed. And as the world stood on the brink of the 1990s nobody, except for a carefully chosen few, had any idea of the extraordinary events that were about to envelop the world.

The Hegarty children win first prize at the annual Dog Tongue Pulling Contest at Crufts.

The 1990s: Back to the Future

The 1990s began with 1990. Mrs Thatcher was sensationally sacked by the Tories when the whole of the parliamentary party suddenly realised that they couldn't stick her. One senior backbencher was quoted as saying "Better no leader at all than her" and with the election of John Major that's exactly what the country got.

In June 1991, Mrs Mary Stupid was enjoying the sun in her back garden when she had a weird visitation. A mysterious hooded figure suddenly appeared from behind the greenhouse. The hooded figure spoke: "Mrs Stupid, I represent a higher power. You have been chosen from billions to relay an important message to mankind."

"Hang on a minute," said Mrs Stupid, "I'll just get a pen and paper." She dashed into the kitchen and returned to the garden a few moments later. She was astonished to discover that not only had the hooded figure disappeared but it had also run off with her lawnmower.

The Eiffel Tower is systematically destroyed in 1994 when the French suddenly realise that they are sick and tired of it.

After the disaster of the 1993 Grand National, the 1994 event is organised on totally different lines.

In sport the world of horse racing suffered a tremendous blow to its confidence when the staging of the 1993 Grand National proved to be a total fiasco. The official inquiry reported that, "It was a very confusing day all round. We were going about our normal business when all of a sudden these horses turned up. And for some bizarre reason each one of them had a little man in colourful clothes sitting on its back. And then, if you please, they all decided that they wanted to race. We can't really be expected to stage a proper Grand National with this kind of behaviour going on." If the world of sport thought it had suffered its worst ever humiliation, it was right. But worse was to follow. In mid-1993 Mrs Stupid was once again sitting in her garden enjoying the bright sunshine when the mysterious hooded figure reappeared from behind a privet hedge. "Mrs Stupid," it said, "time is running away from us."

"Where's my lawnmower?" said Mrs Stupid.

"Ah yes, your lawnmower," replied the mysterious hooded figure. "Let me explain. I am from another world and we know so little of your engineering skills. I took your lawnmower so that the Elders could understand its complicated

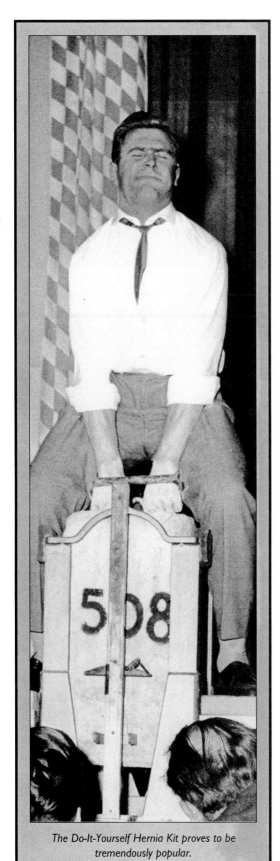

The Do-It-Yourself Hernia Kit *proves to be tremendously popular.*

machinery. But I have a message for you. A message you must convey to your fellow man."

"Hang on." said Mrs Stupid, "I'll just get a pen and paper." When she returned, Mrs Stupid was absolutely flabbergasted to discover that not only had the mysterious hooded figure disappeared, but so had her garden chairs and wishing well.

The latest fashion craze hits Europe. Suddenly insects everywhere start wearing human faces on their feet.

In 1994 the F A Cup Final between Stoke City and Manchester United was reduced to a nonsense when, shortly after the two teams had been introduced to the Duchess of Kent, it was realised that nobody had thought to bring a football. The Duchess attempted to save the day by volunteering

Dr Heinrich Stupid-Name relaxing at home.

her handbag as a replacement, (**above**) but the players were eventually called off the pitch after twenty minutes when the straps fell off. For the television viewers this was a blessed relief because the commentators had made a terrible mess of re-adapting their terminology to fit the new circumstances – "And Hancock has split United's defence with a marvellous through handbag" was just one of the many phrases that made viewers wince in their armchairs.

Although sport was having a rough time, scientists all over the place were making startling breakthroughs. In 1995, DNA cloning was perfected by Dr Heinrick Stupid-Name who astonished the world by recreating Elvis Presley as he was when he was 23 years old (**below**). Elvis immediately embarked on a world tour including Britain and received standing ovations everywhere with his vibrant performances of all the old rock and roll classics. He weighed 11½ stone.

In that same year, Mrs Stupid was again sunbathing in her garden when the mysterious hooded figure suddenly rose out of the ornamental pond. As it brushed a couple of water lilies off its hood Mrs Stupid angrily demanded the return of her garden chairs and wishing well. "And furthermore," she continued, "I've got a pen and paper right here, so if you have got an important message for humanity you might as well give it to me at dictation speed."

"I see," replied the mysterious hooded figure, "but first I must anoint you with this magic wand." The mysterious hooded figure then whacked Mrs Stupid across the back of the head with a length of lead piping. When she recovered consciousness some seven hours later, Mrs Stupid immediately noticed that somebody had stolen her ornamental pond.

In 1996 rocket scientists invented a special new fuel that made it possible for human beings to fly to the moon inside twenty four minutes. Not only was the journey quick but it was cheap as well. I myself journeyed to the moon in 1996 where the photograph on the front cover of this book was taken.

Towards the end of 1996, political commentators were completely taken by surprise when Steven Spielberg became President of the United States (**below**). Many astute observers of the political scene had predicted that his opponent, Roy the chocolate egg, would win by a landslide. His campaign slogan had been much admired for its direct simplicity – "Vote for Roy – He's a chocolate egg!" But Spielberg had enthused the American people with his personal vision of the future. "Science is making extraordinary discoveries," he told them, "I believe we are on the brink of developing a very special pill that will cure every single major disease and it may even reverse the ageing process. These are very important times.

In the late 1990s Siamese twins show that they still know how to enjoy themselves.

The millennium is nearly upon us and we need somebody in charge who isn't a chocolate egg. And if I become President I will do my utmost to persuade the Beatles to reform." And when he became President, he did.

On January 28th 1997, the three ex-Beatles, Paul McCartney, George Harrison and Ringo Starr were pacing nervously backstage at the Hollywood Bowl when a recently-created John Lennon clone walked into their dressing room. A fist fight immediately broke out. This seemed to clear the air and the four mop-tops sat down to work out a running order. John was reluctant to perform *Ebony and Ivory* and so another fist fight broke out (**right**). Paul eventually conceded that they shouldn't sing *Ebony and Ivory* as long as they also didn't perform *Imagine*, which he described undiplomatically as "a tuneless dirge". There seemed to be general agreement over this until another fist fight broke out. Eventually, battered and bruised, the Beatles took to the stage and easily surpassed everybody's ludicrously high expectations. The concert was filmed using a special new three dimensional process that allowed their fans to watch the entire performance over and over again in the form of a life-size hologram. It sold 300 million copies within its first few hours of release.

By the end of 1998 scientific advances were rapidly changing the world. Crops were growing in deserts, world economies were flourishing and the holes in the

ozone layer were repaired with a special new ozone replacement substance. The British Prime Minister, Sir David Mellor (**left**), announced that, for the first time in its history, Britain enjoyed full employment; apart from one man in Leeds who apparently had a bit of a bad back.

On June 21st 1999, Mrs Mary Stupid turned up at the White House demanding to see President Spielberg. She told the security men about her mysterious visitations and that she had an important message to convey to mankind. She was of course immediately ushered into the Oval Office. She told the President her story and informed him that ever since she had been whacked across the back of the head, she had been hearing strange voices on a daily basis. After listening carefully, the President said, "I believe you." He then produced a satellite photograph from the top right hand drawer of his desk. The photograph, which had been taken some five hundred miles above the earth's surface, clearly

showed six rather unusual objects circling the globe. Mrs Stupid immediately recognised her lawnmower, her ornamental pond, her garden chairs and her wishing well (**right**).

At 11.57pm on December 31st 1999 television programmes all over the world were simultaneously interrupted by a short burst of interference. Then Mrs Mary Stupid appeared. "To cut a long story short," she said, "I have been in contact with aliens from another world. They have asked me to tell you to go outside. They want you all to stand outside your front doors or your mud huts or your igloos and look up to the sky." As one, the people of the world did as they were told. They looked up to the sky and gasped at the extraordinary display of colours dancing above them. They saw coloured shapes, shapeless colours, deep

rich colours, transparent colours and brand new colours that swirled around and between all the other colours. And each man, woman and child pointed up to the sky eager to pick out some detail that their friends or family may have missed. And as the clocks struck twelve a warm tingling sensation flooded through their minds and bodies. They all suddenly realised that, without exception, everybody in the world was pointing. And it felt great.

This time traveller arrived from the 23rd century in 1997 and immediately landed a job as a keep fit expert on breakfast television.

Later that morning, as people drifted back inside they discovered, much to their amusement, that somebody had stolen all their furniture. All except for one item. And so, without really knowing why, that night each citizen of the world took turns to sprawl across the table.

THE END

Author's note: In the year 2002 the "Bring Back the Twentieth Century Society" was formed.

P.S.

It is just feasible that you may have found some of the historical facts in this book somewhat questionable, but simply by looking back through the book at the photographs seen below, you will realise that the authority with which my account has been written stems from my own first-hand experience of the events I have described.

I was there.

page 29

page 11

page 15

page 38

page 54

page 50

page 66

page 80

page 76

page 88